The Beauty of New Zealand

The Beauty of New Zealand

Robin Smith
Warren Jacobs

with text by Errol Brathwaite

Golden Press

AUCKLAND CHRISTCHURCH SYDNEY

Lake Quill and the Sutherland Falls

Rugged mountains, graceful lakes and snow-fed rivers

To say that New Zealand contains mountains, lakes and rivers would be a gross understatement. Mountains, lakes and rivers in this country are not mere features, but the very shape and essence of the land—forces which play their part in shaping, not only the rest of the non-mountainous and non-riparian New Zealand landscape, but the very character of the country and its peoples. It must be unique, this mere 270 000 square kilometres, in possessing both a variety of scenery which represents practically every type of landscape to be found anywhere in the world, and a population of under 3 000 000 which exhibits a number of regional characteristics.

The old Maori legend has it that the demigod, Maui, went out in a canoe with his brothers, fishing. Maui caught a monstrous fish, hauling it to the surface, whereupon his brothers, catchless and ravenously hungry, leaped on to it and began to eat it there and then. It lies there still, beside the canoe, all slashed and gnawed, with its great backbone exposed.

This 'backbone' begins with the Coromandel Range, high hills rather than mountains, by New Zealand standards, with no peaks of more than 1 000 metres in height. It continues down the Kaimai Range, appears as odd chains of 'vertibrae' on the central volcanic plateau, knots into a tangle of peaks where the Kaimanawas dovetail into the Ruahine Range, and continues, with occasional peaks of almost 2 000 metres, to the Manawatu Gorge, where they are chopped through by the river, on whose right bank the Ruahines terminate in sheer faces and steep

slopes, and on whose left bank the Tararua Range rises abruptly and continues in an unbroken chain of 1 000 to 1 700 metre peaks to the head of the 'fish'.

The 'canoe', of course, is the South Island, and has its own mighty mountain chain, higher and grander than the mountains of the North Island, especially along that sector of the massif known as the Southern Alps. Highest of these alpine peaks is Mount Cook named by the Maoris *Aorangi*, the Cloud Piercer, thrusting up to 3,762 metres; and there are more than a hundred and thirty peaks that rise over 2 400 metres.

The South Island mountains have grown slowly, so that rivers have here and there cut into them as they grew. Clearly the volcanic mountains had a very different origin. Where they stand, the entire landscape tends to be dotted with other, similar but smaller swellings, or rent with ancient fissures, and oddly terraced. Rivers have a way of sliding peacefully along a forest floor, to leap suddenly into space and fall into a basin of tortured rock thirty metres below. Lakes on the volcanic plateau tend to be gigantic subsidences, like Taupo, a sheet of extremely deep water 616 square kilometres in area.

The volcanic cones themselves are sometimes beautifully symmetrical. Egmont, for instance, the 2 520-metre dormant volcano on the West Cape of the North Island, is sometimes referred to as New Zealand's Fuji, although its symmetry is somewhat marred by the humped shoulder of Fantham's Peak, which juts out on its southern side. Ngauruhoe, in the centre of the island, is

Lake Mangamahoe and Mount Egmont

Mount Egmont is usually referred to as an extinct volcano. It is actually a dormant volcano, according to vulcanologists.

Balfour Glacier, Mount Cook

One of many glaciers on the slopes of
New Zealand's highest mountain, the
Balfour is fed by the eternal snowfields on
the precipitous flanks of the great pinnacle.
A gleaming river of ice, it is typical of the
scenic splendour of this region.

Mount Cook from Hooker Valley

Mount Cook has been climbed frequently,
though even the easiest routes to the
summit are only for experienced climbers.
This approach leads up the Hooker Valley
to the Hooker Glacier.

Mount Cook, above and opposite

Highest peak in the Southern Alpine chain,
Mount Cook soars 3 762 metres, its massive,
sheer faces perpetually snow-covered and
continuously shedding snow in great,
crashing avalanches. Weather from the
west piles up behind its mighty shoulders, in
the form of a boiling, porridge-like mass of
cloud which seethes and rises under the
pressure of powerful winds, to slop over
the ridges and spill down into the Tasman
Valley. From the darkness at the head of

Lake Pukaki, where the Tasman Valley
opens out into the Mackenzie Basin, the top
of Mount Cook appears to catch fire as the
first rays of the morning sun strike it; and
from that moment on, it presents a
breathtaking display of light, shade, colour
and changing mood throughout the day.

another near-perfect cone, though it is entangled in a rent and heaped clutter of peaks and ridges. Its two neighbours, Ruapehu and Tongariro, are not particularly symmetrical at all; or, rather, Ruapehu is, especially from a distance, a shapely cone, but proves to be so rifted with gullies and spurred with minor ridges, as to have the appearance, from some angles, of the skeleton of a cone. Tongariro is a torn, shattered peak, all steaming ponds, boiling streams and fumaroles.

There are other volcanic peaks dotted here and there throughout the country. Pirongia Mountain, in the Waikato, still manages to appear awesomely shattered, despite its softening drapery of rain forest; and the city of Auckland is set on a series of more-or-less perfect minor cones across the Tamaki Peninsula, with the perfectly symmetrical Rangitoto Island guarding the approach to the harbour from the Hauraki Gulf.

In the South Island, Banks Peninsula is a ripped and blasted collection of volcanic cones, the two largest of which blew out with titanic force in recent times, geologically speaking, letting in the sea to form Lyttelton and Akaroa Harbours. From Christchurch, the chain of hills which separate the city from its port are, like Pirongia Mountain, jaggedly shattered, without the softening effect of trees to hide the distorted lava plugs along the crest. From the air, the ancient lava flows can still be seen as they froze, creeping out across the plain and into Lake Ellesmere.

The South Island's alpine chain, structurally similar to the central ranges of the North Island, but on a grander scale, stretches in a more-or-less unbroken wall, from the

Arrow Basin and Remarkables

The Arrow River, rising in the Harris Mountains, snakes through a narrow valley, carved by some ancient glacier, to join the Kawarau not far from Lake Wakatipu. The turbulent stream is fed by little rain- and snow-fed rills, forming a natural irrigation system, greening the Arrow Basin and making it an hospitable area, easy to live in by comparison with the surrounding, desert-like country. The Arrow River was the scene of a massive gold-rush in the 1860s.

drowned valleys which form the Marlborough Sounds, to the sunken glacial valleys which form the Fiords of South Westland. There are branching chains, notably the Kaikouras, the Humboldt Mountains, the Darran Range, the Dart Barrier Range and the Remarkables. The Alps are monstrous serrations, holding long, serpentine lakes entrapped in their folds, and giving birth, in secret valleys, to fierce, snow-fed rivers. The central chain of peaks rears up from a maze of high ridges whose feet are lost in primeval, olive-drab beech forest, which, in some areas and at lower altitudes, gives way to tracts of *totara* and *rimu*, splashed, here and there in due season, with the scarlet of *rata* blossom and the gold of *kowhai*, with, in places, great clouds of yellow where exotic larch turns colour in the early autumn frosts.

The whole area is one of breathtaking beauty, Nature presenting vista after vista of stupendous, snow-mantled heights framed in exquisite sylvan beauty.

But the mountains are crumbling. The lower peaks, which lose their snow in summer, stand revealed as gargantuan gravel heaps—with rocky skeletons, to be sure, but with their mighty flanks eroding at a rate which keeps the long Canterbury rivers gravel-choked and quite unlike rivers anywhere else in the land.

Canterbury rivers can flood with savage power. They can be deep and treacherous; but over much of their length they are tangled skeins of fierce creeks running over gravel beds, sometimes disappearing beneath the gravel for considerable distances.

It is generally said that rivers on this eastern side of the Alps are slow, gravel-choked and meandering, whereas the West Coast rivers are short, swift and deep. But this is a generalization. There are West Coast rivers which wander pleasantly across pastureland and through forests which are almost subtropically luxuriant; and there are eastern rivers which flow deep, wide and implacable.

The Mawheraiti River, for example, chatters placidly across Westland pastures and weaves its way through heaped dredge tailings. The Clutha, on the other hand, flows out of an alpine lake, swift, deep and pugnacious, brawling through a dun-coloured countryside where the hills have had their tops planed smooth by Ice Age glaciers and where the rock ribs of the mountains show through the patchy grass; through rock-bound gorges it punches its way, out to lush lowland pastureland where the willows trail long, green fingers in its green water, and only the occasional whirlpools and eddies show how deep and swift the green water is. It divides to flow around a wide, low-lying island before joining up again and surging into the Pacific Ocean. Navigable, though seldom navigated now, it is New Zealand's greatest river in terms of volume of water. And it is swift and strong, all the way from the mountains.

New Zealand's longest river is the Waikato, also navigable for small boats, and also rarely navigated. The only river still navigated to any extent is the Wanganui, which winds through pastoral country, native bushland, past Maori settlements; the paddle steamer and houseboat trips up and downstream have been discontinued, and the best a tourist can now do is to take a jet-boat trip a few kilometres upstream from Taumaranui.

Jet-boat trips are also available on Canterbury's Waimakariri, in the South Island. Indeed, the jet-boat is a Canterbury invention, and a necessity for people who wish to navigate those great tangles of waterways where the maximum allowable draught is apt to be about one and a half centimetres. There is much deep water in the Waimakariri, particularly in the Waimakariri Gorge, where the river emerges from the high country and rushes between restricting rock walls and past pockets of native bush and small, sandy beaches; and it is this part of the trip which makes it worthwhile, for the initial stages consist of a series of twisting runs over shallow rapids, between gorse-crowned shingle banks —a noisy and rather dull proceeding, perhaps even a little alarming for people who are not

Clinton Canyon, Milford Track ▶

Clinton Canyon is a narrow, rock-walled
defile through which you climb up to
Mackinnon Pass, past the exquisite Lake
Mintaro, fed by the mad Clinton River
which rushes down from its 395 metre-high
source over a short twenty-two kilometre
run.

Ocean Peak and Mount Emily ▼

used to speeding through puddle-deep water.

New Zealand's lakes offer the best inland boating. Taupo, as has been described, is an inland sea, over 500 square kilometres of usually placid water which can, however, whip up on occasion to a dangerous turbulence. Willow-lined and hill-girt, its beaches strewn with pumice, (that curious, floating volcanic stone), its water temperate enough for comfortable and enjoyable swimming, teeming with trout, lying within easy reach of all the more interesting geothermal areas, it tends to be both a tourist mecca and a favourite holiday spot for New Zealanders themselves. In some areas, this attraction for the domestic holiday-makers can be a drawback, because the landscape tends to become dotted with ill-designed, jerry-built holiday houses. Taupo stood in some danger of this towards the end of the 1940s, when increasing affluence and improved roads placed it within the reach of many more people than had hitherto been the case; but intelligent town planning and careful control ensured that holiday and residential development did not spoil the sylvan beauty of the lake's shores.

The same sort of control has been applied too late to some of the southern lakes, those broad, mountain-walled, wandering sheets of water, 200 to 250 square kilometres in area, 300 metres deep, the remnants of Ice Age glaciers trapped where the ice sheet receded. Typical of these, and perhaps the most beautiful, is Wakaṭipu (properly Wakatipua, 'the Trench of the Demon'), at the centre point of which is Queenstown, a tiny alpine village which still retains considerable charm. There are settlements of scruffy baches here and there, while the best of the original buildings are being swept away, and the most incongruous modern styles appearing in the form of holiday houses and motels. But the lake itself, and its mountain surroundings, are breathtakingly beautiful and almost unspoilable. To look across the Frankton Arm at the Remarkables on a clear night when the snow on those striated faces reflects the moonlight, or

Bottom, snow-laden trees

The maze of ridges from which the great central peaks of the Southern Alps rise are clothed, at their lower altitudes, with native beech forest. There are, however, highland areas where there is little or no native growth, and here, man-made forests and shelter belts of hardy northern hemisphere conifers, firm the crumbling slopes. These firs thrive in areas where snow covers the ground for six months of the year, and incidentally lend to New Zealand ski slopes a flavour of Switzerland.

Top: Coronet Peak Ski Huts and Car Park

Coronet Peak is one of the venues for major ski sports competitions in New Zealand, (the other being Ruapehu, in the North Island) and the excellent, clear slopes, covered with snow for seven or eight months in a good year, attract skiers from all over the world.

Mackinnon Pass and Mount Balloon, Milford Track ▶

Billed with some justification as the most famous walk in the world, the Milford Track winds through the mountains from the head of Lake Te Anau. The way takes the tramper through the awesome Clinton Canyon and up over the Pass beneath some of the country's most stupendous peaks. The walk takes three days, with overnight stops at Pompolona and Quintin Huts, and brings you to Milford Sound.

Pyramid Hills, Lindis ▼

Brown, desert-like countryside encloses the Lindis Pass, where a road runs through from Queenstown and the Southern Lakes to the Mackenzie Basin. For all its brown, burnt appearance, and its snows in winter and fierce heat in summer, it is productive sheep country.

Opposite left: Lake Taupo Sunrise

Across Lake Taupo's 616 square kilometres, the three volcanoes of Tongariro National Park rise up above a scarf of early morning mist, and a cirrus sky promises a glorious day. Taupo abounds in trout, and this is one of its principal attractions for holiday makers.

Glendhu Bluff and Diamond Lake ▼

Glowering over Glendhu Bay on Lake Wanaka, Glendhu Bluff is a terraced, hummocky hill, in a fold in one of whose terraces is Diamond Lake, a still, mirror-like mere in a golden-brown, forest-patched fastness, a miniature of Lake Wanaka itself, overhung by the gargantuan Cosmos Peaks.

Opposite right: Remarkables, Sunset

The rugged faces of the Remarkables Range are a favourite subject for painters. Throughout the day, they present a fascinating interplay of light and shadow and changing colours; and as the sun begins to disappear behind the bulk of Queenstown's western mountain wall, and the shadow climbs up the Remarkables, the last rays of sunlight paint the jagged rocks in delicate shades of pink, against a darkening eastern sky.

to stroll through the streets at the top of the ancient terminal moraine on which the town is built, and feel the frost already in the air of an autumn afternoon when the sun has gone down behind the mountains, and the smoke from the chimneys clings to the steep, pine-covered hill, and the hawthorn and briar hips glow red-hot against the tinted hedges, is an experience which fills the mind with quiet. One is apt to forget that such peaceful, sublime beauty still exists in a raucous world.

Like the rivers and the mountains, the lakes of New Zealand vary widely in character. Within a stone's throw of Lake Wakatipu is Lake Hayes, a willow-bordered water which could have been lifted bodily, complete with the hills immediately surrounding it, from England's Lake District; within a day's easy driving, there is Wanaka, to the north, with its pleasant beaches, its brown hills and enchanting vistas of distant, snowy peaks; and to the south, Te Anau, with its deep fiords, its cave-pierced mountains; and Manapouri, forest-wrapped and dotted with forested islands.

New Zealand's mountain chains have divided the country into clearly definable areas, whose people possess certain characteristics and particular outlooks.

The Southern Alps for many years kept the people of Westland virtually isolated from the rest of the country. Westland was originally settled by miners, seeking gold initially and finding it in reasonably large quantities, and mining for coal latterly. Denied ready contact with the solid Church of England settlers of Canterbury, they became a self-sufficient people. West Coasters are a friendly,

Remarkables and Kawarau River

Leaning back from the centre reach of Lake Wakatipu, in the southern mountains, the Remarkables Range is typical of Central Otago high country. There is no softness, no tree-clad gentleness about these mountains. Here the bare rock ribs of the land are exposed, harsh and jagged. But on a moonlit night, the snow casts a reflected light over the lake; and when the late afternoon sun slants down, in the moments before it sinks behind the ranges, the tops of the Remarkables are tinged with rose pink, turning slowly to coldly-beautiful shadings and touches of blue.

17

open-handed people, apt to be rough in manner and speech. Yet they are, as often as not, an erudite people, placing a high value on education, both for the nourishment of the mind, (particularly important in a situation where the only diversion or entertainment available was that which they made for themselves), and for the acquisition of the kind of knowledge which enabled them to tame and control their wild environment.

The high-country people of the South Island, whatever their antecedents, are true highlanders. It would be impossible to live amongst those towering peaks, and through those white winters and burning summers without gaining an immense self-sufficiency coupled with a humility born of an overwhelming sense of one's relative size in the scheme of things. High-country people are independent, and readily acknowledge it. In powerful country, you have to know someone very well indeed before you rely on him to any vital extent, and therefore they do not readily admit outsiders into their close fellowship. Not that they are taciturn or unfriendly, as a general rule: they seem to have the gift of quietness without being sombre.

Mirror Lakes and Mount Eglinton ▲

The Mirror Lakes are small pools on the side of the road which runs from Lake Te Anau to Milford Sound. Still and sheltered, they reflect the surrounding mountains like polished glass. Mount Eglinton, and indeed, all the peaks in this area, are at their most beautiful after rain, when they are laced with hundreds of waterfalls, most of which disappear after a couple of hours of dry weather.

◀ The Fox Glacier

The sixteen-kilometre Fox Glacier descends on the western side of the Main Divide, from shelves of perpetual snow to gorgeously-forested hills. On the banks of the Fox River, which emerges from an ice cave at the terminal face of the glacier, are hot springs which trickle over moraine gravel to join the chill, smoky-coloured melt-water.

Queenstown from Skyline ▲

Town Hill, as the great hump which looms over the little town is prosaically named, is surmounted by the Skyline Chalet, a restaurant, access to which is by way of a cableway. From this lofty eyrie, a glorious view is obtained of the great Lake Wakatipu, the Remarkables Range, and, right underfoot, tiny Queenstown, with its narrow streets, its enchanting Gardens on the peninsula across Town Bay, and its 'suburb' of Kelvin Heights, on the bush-clad promontory in the middle distance.

Tree Ferns and Bush, Coromandel ▶

Typical of northern rain forest, this scene is one of almost tropical luxuriance. The tree ferns grow prolifically throughout most of the country, the tallest species attaining heights of around ten metres. Their lighter green fronds contrast gently with the overall dark, olive-green foliage of the forest, and the splashes of scarlet *rata*.

Lake Tarawera ▼

'Tarawera' means 'the Hot Peak', and the name was originally that of a nearby mountain, which exploded with titanic force on 10 June 1886, and threw hot rocks and ash all over the surrounding countryside, burying a small tourist village near the lake itself. Lake Tarawera is now a still and beautiful water, lapping the feet of the riven mountain. Spectacular native bush comes right down to its edge, standing back here and there to make room for a narrow curve of sandy beach. There are ancient Maori rock paintings on the Te Wairoa (Buried Village) shore, and Buried Village itself has been partially excavated.

Autumn, Lake Wanaka ▶

The wider areas, the stretches of country which are veined with close networks of roads, produce people who, if they have local characteristics, soon lose them. It is still true that people in Auckland are generally akin to Australians in outlook and accent, and that the people of Invercargill, in the deep south, are generally Scottish in attitude and speech. But these differences are not as sharply defined as they were even twenty years ago. There is a shading. The hills, which used to isolate settlements, have been tamed by good, high-speed roads. The new affluence of the second half of the twentieth century has given people more leisure for travelling, and has given a feeling of security which enables them to pack up and move about the country, confident there will always be work and somewhere to live when they arrive at their destination. So New Zealanders in these areas are a restless people, moving where the work is, not forming strong attachments to any locality—at least not to the extent of yearning to stay in it or return to it.

But there are still barriers. The man who grew up in the limestone hills of Hawkes Bay probably prefers that country to the flatness and, to him, monotony of the Canterbury Plains; but he does not find life there so very different, nor the people so very dissimilar, to those he knew in his home province. But the low-country man or the plainsman finds alpine country too hard, and the cruel peaks leaning over him too oppressive, and rarely settles in the highlands.

The Central Otago man conceives a great love for his brown land with its numbing winter frosts and its desert heat in summer. Those dry, rock-ribbed hills, with the harrier hawks wheeling on the updraughts of heated valley air, and the little green hollows with friendly stone houses and shivering poplars which occasionally delight the eye in that vastness, lay hold upon him. He is, or tends to be, a man with a gift for silences, sharing that characteristic with the high-country man. Both are hospitable, gregarious within their own environment and amongst their own people, just as the Westlanders are. And, somehow, everyone else is an outsider, in spite of the courtesy and friendliness they'll show him.

Lake Moeraki ▲

Lake Moeraki is southernmost of the exquisite South Westland lakes. Framed in bush, abounding in trout, and overlooked by the Thomas Range, it is really a broadening of the Moeraki River, six and a half square kilometres in area, and about four and a quarter metres deep at its deepest point. The surrounding forest is the haunt of deer and wild pig, and in the trees at the lake's edge may sometimes be seen *kotuku*, the Sacred White Heron. Moeraki derives its name from a type of potato, which the lake is supposed to resemble in shape.

Whangarei Falls and Forest, Northland ▶

There is none of the awe-inspiring, brutal power possessed by many New Zealand falls to be seen in the Whangarei Falls. They are memorable for the delicate, veil-like quality of the draped water, and the sylvan loveliness of the setting. The stratification of the rock hints at titanic forces in an agonized volcanic past; but the gentle moss and shading bush, and the veil of water soothe away the last whisper of ancient fire and hurt. The Whangarei Falls are typical of Northland, where all the features found in the rest of New Zealand are reproduced on a smaller, more manageable scale.

◄ Lake Matheson, Westland

Close to the terminal face of the Fox Glacier, Lake Matheson represents the glacier's farthest reach, before a warming climate forced it to retreat back to the foot of the mountains. The lake is the melted remains of a huge block of dead ice. Surrounded by exquisite native bush, sheltered from the wind, its surface is mirror-like, and acoustics in that still area are such as to give the bird-song from the surrounding forest a quality of unearthly beauty.

Lake Hayes ▼

Lake Hayes is a small lake set in scenes of pastoral beauty, an almost surprising phenomenon so close to the vertical and harshly alpine landscape of Wakatipu, which is a mere stone's throw away. Lake Hayes is so abundant in trout that the fishing season is from October till the end of August, with an enormous limit bag. The locality is at its most beautiful in autumn, (end of March, first half of April), when the early frosts are turning the leaves of the poplars a bright yellow, and the hawthorn hedges are aglow with berries.

Papakorito Falls, Lake Waikaremoana ►

Lake Waikaremoana, in the Urewera Highlands, is a gem of other-worldly beauty. Formed in no very remote period by the collapse of a hillside and the consequent blocking of a river valley, it spreads, blue and island-dotted, over some fifty-three square kilometres. It is fed by streams which drain nearly 340 square kilometres of densely wooded, rugged country, streams which leap down mountainsides in a series of exquisite cascades. Papakorito Falls are near a track known as the Old Gisborne Road. Some fifteen metres in height, they form lacy tiers, spreading out in a smooth flare before plunging into the basin at the foot of the three-stepped bluff.

Huka Falls, Waikato River ►

The Huka Falls are noted, not for their height, for they are by no means lofty, but for the savage power of their green, foaming water. Viewpoints have been established along the eastern bank, securely railed, and are reached by means of a suspension bridge which crosses the river close to the actual cataract.

It is the mountains that make these people different. It is as though mountains are the only real barriers, the only features which have that property of fencing people in, and allowing them to develop independently.

New Zealand's mountain regions are inhabited; not in the way that the Swiss Alps are inhabited, or the slopes of Vesuvius, or even the American Ozarks. They are sparsely inhabited by hunters, who cull the forest-damaging deer, spending the greater part of their working lives in the steep bush. They are inhabited by the people who run mountain resorts, and who guide, and who teach climbers and skiers; but almost every New Zealander spends some time in them. They can come to grips with the mountains, living for a day or two in the shade of their stupendous peaks and shadowy gorges, tramping around their still tarns and trudging up long ridges. They can climb to the tops of the glaciers—the Tasman, the Murchison, the Fox which curves upwards into the snowy plateaux on the western side of the Alps, and the Franz Josef which, like the Fox, descends from snowfields to terminate in native bush of sub-tropical luxuriance.

Many New Zealanders, and many visitors, climb the Alps, and ski on fields like Coronet Peak, near Queenstown, or the slopes of

Ruapehu and Egmont. There are smaller fields with more primitive facilities, such as the Tararua skifield in the North Island's Wairarapa, north-east of Wellington, and Powdersnow Valley, cradled high on the flank of Mount Potts, at Erewhon, not two hours' drive from Christchurch.

The fact is that few New Zealanders live out of sight of snow-capped ranges, or out of reach of vast lakes and clean rivers. These things are commonplace, the New Zealander's heritage. He accepts them casually, and regards them as a prized but permanent possession.

Lake Middleton, Ohau

Lake Middleton is a typical high-country lake, as distinct from those trapped glacial lakes in the midst of the mountains. They are of two kinds—snow-fed and rain-fed—distinguishable from each other by their colour. (Snow-fed lakes appear from the air as lapis-lazuli blue, somewhat opaque, whereas rain-fed lakes are green-clear). The surrounding country is characteristic of the Mackenzie Basin, with its brown snowgrass, its briars and spiny *matagouri* scrub, and its clumps of dark pines, splashed in autumn with the yellow of larch.

Arrowtown Avenue

Arrowtown is one of the few gold-rush settlements which have changed very little over the years, and which are still lived in. There are new houses here, and a new pub, but many of the houses, standing back behind the trees in avenues such as this, are original miners' cottages, updated only in the matter of internal plumbing, heating arrangements and electricity.

Glendhu Bay ▼

Glendhu Bay, on Lake Wanaka, is one of the bays from which holiday crowds swim. Even in the considerable heat of summer, however, the water is very cold, and the swimming season is apt to be short. In autumn, Glendhu Bay becomes a favourite spot for trout fishermen, who catch both brown and rainbow trout in Lake Wanaka, as well as Atlantic salmon, which grow in these waters to not much more than two and a half kilograms.

◀ *Head of Lake Wakatipu, Otago*

This ancient, trapped glacier is a water of superlative beauty. In this view, the Humboldt Mountains begin to rise on the left, and Mount Earnslaw appears on the right. Over the low spur where a mountain sheep station comes down to the water, the Dart River flows into the Lake.

Church of the Good Shepherd, Lake ▼
Tekapo

Lake Tekapo, eighty-three square kilometres in area, lies at an altitude of 720 metres. On the fringe of the Mackenzie Country, it is a popular resort for boating, water skiing and fishing in summer, and for skiers in winter. The Mackenzie Country is an alpine basin, notable for sheep-raising, and derives its name from a sheep stealer, who first perceived its potential in the late 1800s, and proceeded to stock it with other

men's sheep. The little stone Church of the
Good Shepherd is an architectural gem,
obviously belonging to its environment. It
is situated on a low promontory where the
Tekapo River flows out of the lake. The
window over the altar is of clear glass,
framing a superb view of the lake and the
distant, snow-capped mountains.

Bays, harbours, cliffs and coves

For a people who ventured in open, double-hulled, ocean-going canoes across the wild Pacific, the Maoris have since shown remarkably little inclination towards ocean navigation. It isn't particularly surprising, perhaps, in view of the fact that their relatively small, pre-European population had the entire, rich country to cater for their needs. They still built superb canoes, especially the great *waka taua*, the war canoes, often over thirty metres long, marvellously carved at prow and stern. The warriors sailed down the coast in them on warlike forays, and, in one incident, carried them overland, from lake to lake, finally launching them on Lake Rotorua, right in the centre of the North Island, and attacking the local tribe in their Mokoia Island stronghold. But, by and large, they did their travelling on foot, moving overland.

The European settlers, on the other hand, sailed up and down the coasts incessantly. The sea was their best method of communication in the days when every settlement was virtually isolated by dense forest and frequently threatened by hostile Maoris.

Consequently, the rugged New Zealand coasts were well charted from the earliest days of settlement.

As the charts reveal, New Zealand coastal waters can be deceptive. Northland harbours, seen from the open sea as broad, landlocked expanses of calm water, turn out to be shallow, mangrove-fringed stretches of tidal lagoon, with perhaps one medium-draught channel snaking through them. Banks Peninsula, and other deeply indented coastlines, are notched with bays that look exactly like nearby harbour entrances, and are in consequence and with grim humour, named

Taylor's Mistake, Murray's Mistake and after a good many other mariners' errors and tragic misjudgments.

But much of the coastline is well provided with deep bays and landlocked coves which make the country a small-boatman's dream.

Types of coastal scenery vary widely, even over a comparatively short length of coast. Within the Bay of Islands, for example, there are golden-sand beaches, gravel beaches, mangrove-tangled tidal mud flats, *pohutukawa*-splashed bush standing directly over the water, huge pinnacles of sea-sculpted rock and miniature estuaries.

Tauranga, 480 kilometres down the east coast from the Bay of Islands, spreads itself around a broad bay pitted with coves and sheltered by the long, low mass of Matakana Island. Many of its coves are strongly reminiscent of tropical isles, with their golden-sand beaches and spits, and white pleasure-craft riding serenely in the shade of palm-like treeferns.

There are drab, grey shingle beaches, such as those which lie along the Napier foreshore, swept by strong currents, steeply shelving and dangerous; or south of Banks Peninsula, at Birdlings Flat, where the fierce rip has torn at the volcanic cliffs and deposited gemstones profusely along the steep and perilous shingle bank which separates Lake Ellesmere from the Pacific Ocean.

Some of the world's finest seascapes are to be found in New Zealand, such as the glorious view from Florence Hill, in the Catlins District of South Otago, where a vast sweep of forest-fringed beach ends where the green and delightful Tautuku Peninsula thrusts out into the empty sea.

Mahurangi Peninsula, North Auckland

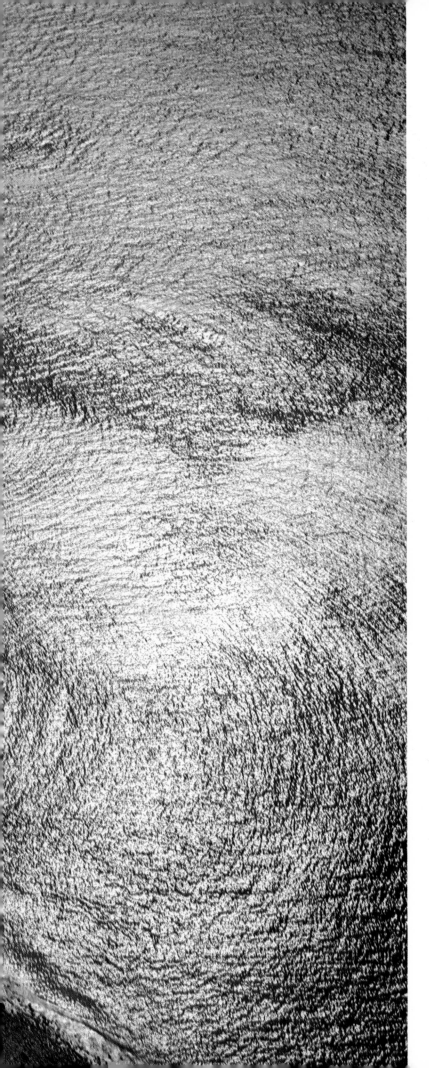

In the south-west are the fiords, drowned glacial valleys cutting far into the mountainous bulk of the land, walled by peaks which climb vertically to the sky from the water's edge, or by gentler but still steep slopes clad in dark, untrodden forest where the mornings are greeted by the chiming of a million bellbirds.

On the western side of the North Island, the great, carved bluffs of Tongaporutu, bush-crowned and frowning, give way gradually to the black ironsand beaches of northern Taranaki, backed by steep gulley-riven slopes, a stern landscape, seen from the sea, but full of bush-clad, bird-haunted beauty, over which Mount Egmont broods silently; and southern Taranaki, flat beyond the hem of Egmont's spreading skirts, lies clifftop-high above buff-coloured sand and sea-gnawed caves.

North-west of Wellington, fine beaches, protected from the rages of the temperamental Tasman Sea by Kapiti and Mana Islands, are interspersed with jagged reefs and bastions of rock; but the beaches narrow perceptibly and the reefs are more frequent as they near Cape Terawhiti at the butt-end of a range of mountainous ridges which drop down abruptly to the turbulent and wind-whipped Cook Strait.

Those rugged ranges once stretched all the way across to Marlborough, in what is now the South Island; but some cataclysmic subsidence snapped the chain at its northern end and dragged the Marlborough mountains down beneath the sea.

Cape Kidnappers Gannet Colony

Lying like the tail of a dragon in a patch of turbulent sea, Cape Kidnappers holds, on a flat and slightly sloping hump, a gannet colony of some 2 800 pairs of these graceful birds, which look like a cross between a pelican and a goose. There are actually two nesting sites, the one shown being accessible to visitors by way of a razor-backed path with steep and rather perilous slopes dropping away on either side.

Their drowned valleys are now magnificent waterways, where high, densely-forested peninsulas and islands organize the sea into a complex of bays and straits, sheltered, deep and teeming with fish. Known as Marlborough Sounds, they reach far inland, the longest arm lapping the feet of the small town of Havelock, and their secluded bays enfolding holiday baches, occasional homes, farms, hotels and guest houses. The beaches, built up over aeons of time, are sometimes sandy, more often golden gravel. The bush echoes all day to the chime of *tui* and bellbirds, and *ruru*, the little bush owl, calls across the glinting water at night.

Westland shores are swept in places by a warm ocean current which, with the sunshine, warms the air between the high Alps and the sea, and produces luxuriant forest, and at least one sandy beach where the tall *nikau* palms add to the tropical aspect of the place. Other Westland beaches are wild and lonely stretches of driftwood-strewn granite sand, reaching around swampy lagoons such as Okarito, where the white heron nests.

New Zealand abounds in good harbours. Auckland's Waitemata is wide and deep, a vast inreaching from the Hauraki Gulf, where the sea wanders up long reaches to mingle with tidal creeks. Its mouth is shielded by the broad, flat cone of Rangitoto, and it is separated from the shallower Manukau by the slim Tamaki Isthmus. Mangroves grow in its shallower arms, and the occasional small, rocky reef and island breaks its sparkling surface. It is a pond-like harbour, mostly, with the land gently sloping down into it— a shallow, drowned valley.

Wellington Harbour, though, is a perfectly land-locked basin, surrounded by high hills. Captain Herd of the barque *Rosanna* wrote in the *Nautical Almanac*, around 1826, that ' . . . here all the navies of Europe might ride in perfect security'.

Lyttelton Harbour, on the northern side of Banks Peninsula, is a long rift, an open-sided crater of a volcanic explosion which would have dwarfed the biggest nuclear bomb yet devised. It is entered through high, embrasured cliffs, where once the guns of shore batteries were emplaced in an antipodean Gibraltar, which now houses seabirds and pigeons. The town of Lyttelton clambers up the inside of the crater wall, flanked by bush-filled fissures and frowned upon by the blasted lava at the rim.

Mitre Peak ▲

Milford Sound is one of the drowned glacial valleys which deeply notch the South Westland coast of the South Island. Deep, bottle-green water and titanic rock walls and forested cliffs rising sheer from the water to heights of 1 500 metres make sailing in these waters an unforgettable experience. Mitre Peak, centre, is one of the highest peaks rising straight out of the water anywhere in the world.

◀ Mount Maunganui

The Mount, as it is affectionately known, is a long, curving beach near Tauranga, in the Bay of Plenty, terminating in a lofty, conical peak, the site of ancient Maori fortifications. The beach is a much favoured venue for competitive surfing.

◀ *Coromandel Peninsula*

The Coromandel Peninsula forms the eastern bastion which shelters the Hauraki Gulf. Hilly and partly forested, its deeply indented shores today provide a number of delightful holiday resorts, golden sand beaches, sheltered and breathtakingly lovely. Coromandel was the scene of a gold strike in 1867, when a reef was discovered which paid handsomely for almost 100 years.

Punakaiki Pancake Rocks ▼

One of Westland's finest beaches, Punakaiki is caressed by a warm ocean current, and the *nikau* palms, the lush, sub-tropical bush which clothes the backdrop of steep ranges, and the smooth sand, make it a favourite and increasingly sought-after holiday place for New Zealanders. The Pancake Rocks are a peculiar geological feature. With the distinct appearance of piles of pancakes, they are pierced by blowholes, through which the inrushing sea fountains upwards, geyser-like, with much subterranean rumbling and sighing.

Opposite: Cape Reinga, Northland

According to Maori lore, Cape Reinga, at the extreme north of the North Island, is the departing place for the spirits of the dead. Here the Tasman Sea and the Pacific ocean meet, in a fierce striving of opposing currents. The sea is a deep blue, shading off to pastel greens near the shore and stitched with lines of white breakers on the reefs. The Maoris say that when a vessel sinks in these seas, a rainbow marks the spot.

Opposite right: Whangaroa Harbour

Whangaroa is typical of Northland's shallow, mangrove-fringed harbours. It winds and twists between high hills, and is looked down upon by two massive rock domes, one on either side, called St Peter's and St Paul's Cupolas. A favourite holiday spot, the Whangaroa provides fine boating water and good fishing.

Opposite left: Hicks Bay, Poverty Bay

Poverty Bay was so named by Captain James Cook because he was unable to obtain either provisions or friendliness from the Maoris in the area, in marked contrast to his reception at the Bay of Plenty, to the north of East Cape.

Moeraki Boulders, Otago

Moeraki Beach is named after the potato which ancient Polynesian voyagers brought with them in their great double-hulled, ocean-going canoe. The canoe, so the olden legend goes, capsized near Shag Point, at the end of the beach, and the *moeraki* potatoes and some gourds which she was carrying were strewn by the tide along the beach, and were later transformed into boulders. Today, these septarian stones lie half buried in sand, a geological oddity, rusty-red or yellow inside, with crystalline cores.

Cape Brett ▼

Cape Brett is the eastern head at the entrance to the Bay of Islands. Hereabouts is a famous big game fishing ground, and the famous Hole in the Rock which is one of the features of special launch cruises, which take passengers through the Hole and into the Grand Cathedral Cave in the vicinity.

The port complex is behind man-made breakwaters and moles, for the prevailing north-east wind comes up the harbour with funnelled force, and its open water can be very rough. The cliffs and bays around the harbour are dotted with pleasant settlements, and the crater itself is old and eroded now, filled at the southern end with the hills and humps formed by the debris of centuries, all grassy and tree-grown.

On the southern side of the peninsula, Akaroa Harbour is similar, but smaller and shallower, with the one-time French settlement of Akaroa clinging to such flat harbourside land as can be found, and wandering up valleys which trend away from the sea, still sentimentally calling its streets Rue Viard and Rue Balguerie and still carefully preserving its quaint French houses with their lacy wrought-iron balconies and their elegant doors and windows.

At the mouth of Akaroa Harbour, and around the north-eastern corner of the peninsula, red volcanic cliffs lean out over the heaving sea, pitted with small caves, the bubbles of the once boiling lava perhaps, or the mouths of fumaroles. Now they are nesting places for shags.

Dunedin Harbour is long and narrow, like Lyttelton, but shallower. The deepest water is at Port Chalmers, near the mouth, a Lyttelton-like town that clambers up the steep hillsides from the water's edge; but a painstakingly dredged channel, carefully marked with buoys and pylons, snakes up to Dunedin itself.

The eastern side of the harbour is the Otago Peninsula. On its ocean shore, there are bays where the kelp swirls around barnacled rocks, and seals bask on offshore islets; and there are sandy inlets with bush-fringed beaches, and caverns where the sea surges in and out and sends strange boomings up deep fissures to the grassy hillsides above. And over all of this enchanting coastline, the ancient lava plugs look down from the hilltops of a timeless sort of land where farms still have drystone fences, and there are houses of grey local stone, and even a castle, the famous Larnach's, from which its builder could spy trading ships approaching the harbour, whereupon he would make haste to have his agents down on the wharf, the first to meet them and the first to pick over their cargoes.

Just as few New Zealanders live out of sight of snow-capped mountain ranges, none lives more than two or three hours' drive from the coast. Beaches, harbours and coves are easily accessible, which is why a boat-building business can thrive in a centre like Fairlie or Taumaranui, which are about as far inland as it is possible to get. New Zealanders are, generally speaking, boating enthusiasts. They are small-boat people, knowledgeable about their home waters, weatherwise because in an

island climate they have to be, and bold, resourceful sailors.

After all, their small-boat tradition goes back a long way, to those missionaries who pottered around uncharted coasts; to the sealers and whalers who felt their way into and out of strange bays and uninhabited fiords, to the Maoris from the Bay of Plenty, who farmed and gardened land in Northland in the early 1800s and traded their produce down the coast in their own fleet of small schooners; and the crayfishers along the Kaikoura Coast today, who nose their craft in and out of some impossibly narrow, monstrously turbulent gut in a kelp-draped, swirl-washed reef, and winch it up at day's end to some shelf which the highest tides and stormiest seas won't reach.

◄ *Castlepoint Lighthouse*

Standing on a bleak spot of the Wairarapa coast, the lighthouse protects shipping from the huge seas that pound the cliffs.

Kaiteriteri Beach ▼

One of the country's most celebrated beaches, Kaiteriteri is a broad crescent of coarse golden sand, sheltered at either end by bush-crowned promontories. Azure water and the drab olive green of beech, with gums and pines standing along the crest of each headland, and the reddish gold of the beach, make it one of the most photogenic beaches. Facing into Golden Bay, and thus protected from the wild winds of the Tasman, it lies as a kind of backwater, by-passed by the swift current of Cook Strait, calm, safe and greatly favoured for boating and swimming, the perfect holiday beach.

◄ Kaikoura

Kaikoura received its name from an ancient Maori explorer, who caught *koura*, the crayfish, here, and enjoyed a meal of it. The name means 'feast of crayfish'. The present-day town is tucked into the foot of the peninsula, where it joins the mainland, and is backed by the magnificent Seaward Kaikoura Range. In this view, showing a reef near the tip of the peninsula in the foreground and the town in its picturesque setting, the sea is in one of its calmer moods, a flat calm with a steely-blue tint to the water. More commonly, in winter, the nor'-east winds whip it into a frenzy, causing great breakers to crash in dense clouds of spume and spray along the rocky coast.

Gog and Magog, Stewart Island ►

Stewart Island, a mountainous island of some 1 700 square kilometres, separated from the southern end of the South Island by one of the roughest stretches of water in the New Zealand territory, is sparsely inhabited, most of the inhabitants being fishermen and their families. It has one township, Oban, beautifully situated in a forest-girt bay. Stewart Island's coastline is rugged, but it possesses beaches and coves of Eden-like beauty, golden sand alternating with silvery sand, often strewn with a scarlet seaweed.

Sandy Bay, Otago ▼

Here the force of the wave patterns of the Great Southern Ocean are deeper felt than any other part of New Zealand. The clear blue water is intensely cold.

There is no such thing as a large commercial fishing fleet in New Zealand, no equivalent of those enormous Japanese trawlers and factory ships which cross the Pacific to fish out a hundred shores. New Zealand commercial fishermen have always fished comparatively close inshore, taking what they need and rather deploring the kind of enterprise which strips a productive area bare.

Fish are becoming hard to find; yet sporting fishermen still make good catches off northern beaches, such as Bayly's Beach, near Dargaville, where local fishermen use a raft, floated out from the beach, laden with baited hooks. They call it a 'galloping gertie'. Birdlings Flat fishermen, in the South Island, use a similar device, called a Kon Tiki, to catch snapper and blue cod.

At the mouths of Canterbury's great rivers, salmon are caught, in season. Anglers often stand a metre or two apart along a tide-and-current-built spit of sand. And on some northern beaches, notably Ninety Mile Beach, (which is actually about half that length), the flat, smooth-washed strip of clean sand backed by the dunes and dune-like hills of the Aupori Peninsula, the *toheroa* is obtained, a large, clam-like shellfish with a flavour as delicate as, but nothing resembling, the finest oysters. *Toheroas*, which make a delicious green soup often favourably compared with turtle soup, are found in only a few localities, and there is a strict limit to the numbers which people may take. In less favoured areas, they make do with the *pipi*, another, smaller clam-like creature which is nevertheless delicious, boiled and eaten with bread and butter and vinegar.

Few districts are not within reach of good surfing and swimming beaches, seashores like Pourerere, in Central Hawkes Bay, where there is more than a kilometre of sandy bottom and huge, crashing Pacific rollers, tamed sufficiently by the broad continental shelf to be safe, powerful enough to provide a thrilling ride shorewards; and there are areas of swimming-pool still water, sheltered by grey *papa* reefs, some of which, completely uncovered at low tide, are veritable marine gardens, their rock pools alive with all manner of fascinating life.

Indeed, there is a great wealth of accessible golden-sand beaches, like those glorious curves backed by steep, forested hills, along the South Otago coast. The water is apt to be cold—a steady 15°C winter and summer—but it teems with fish; and those hills immediately behind the beaches are laced with tumbling forest brooks and waterfalls and lakelets of sublime loveliness. And they're empty, most of those beaches. Their caves, their tall cliffs stratified interestingly with rock and coal, their bared scarps of volcanic conglomerate which looks as crumbly as cheese but is actually hard as ferro-concrete and contains microscopic sapphires and emeralds, products of the fiery alchemy of the world's birth, are visited spasmodically but never crowded. There are beaches to spare.

And they teem with a variety of life, off-shore. The Bay of Islands has its big game fish, the swordfish and the marlin.

Off Kaikoura, seals swim, and whales are not uncommonly observed as they surface briefly and blow; and on the ocean side of the Otago Peninsula, there are beaches where, punctually in the early evening, hordes of penguins surf into the beach, waddle ashore, preen shining wet feathers, and disappear into the tussock and scrub above the beach, to nest for the night.

Queen Charlotte Sound

The network of drowned valleys which form the Marlborough Sounds are poems of placid, deep water and forested peninsulas. Queen Charlotte Sound, with the township and entry-port of Picton at its head, is the busiest, with fishing boats, pleasure craft and the inter-island rail-ferries, *Aramoana* and *Aranui*, plying from the Picton harbour; launch traffic, fishing and carrying supplies and mail for outlying farms, finds its way into all of the waterways.

Cities in search of the best of two worlds

Until recently, there has been very little difference between New Zealand cities and New Zealand small towns, except for the size of the populations. Perhaps the cities have possessed buildings which run to seven or eight storeys, whereas two is about the limit for small towns; but New Zealanders have always been uneasy when deprived of green grass and growing plants, and have clung resolutely to the quarter-acre building section.

Streets and streets of bungalows, usually wooden, mostly single-storeyed, have spread out around a commercial centre with one or more streets of shops and blocks of office buildings; and the inhabitants usually came to the city centre at least once a week to 'do the shops'.

Life in a city has always been, until quite recently, precisely like life in a country town, with the addition of a bus service and a few more theatres, pubs and places of entertainment.

But the change is happening, and happening fast. Across the isthmus of the northern peninsula, lumpy with its ancient volcanic cones, Auckland spreads like a many-coloured cloth. Most cosmopolitan of New Zealand cities, and the largest, (pop. 500 000-plus), Auckland is a lively, bustling place. It still sprawls, and always will, a vast conglomeration of multi-coloured houses. But high-rise buildings are springing up like mushrooms in tight clusters in the city's commercial heart, and new shopping complexes and malls are growing in suburbs which, ten or fifteen years ago, were satellite towns. People in suburbs like Three Kings or Papatoetoe, now inseparably part of Auck-land proper, still shop and live within their own boundaries, just as they always did, because it simply isn't worth while to go across the busy town to the central Queen Street and Karangahape Road areas.

Auckland crowds down to the small, sandy bays of the Waitemata (Sparkling Waters) harbour, which, many branched, serves as the Aucklanders' almost universal playground. The harbour influences their lifestyle profoundly, making of them an outdoor people. It could hardly be otherwise, for they see it every day. Thousands of them cross it, driving or riding in buses over the great Auckland Harbour Bridge, coming from North Shore suburbs to work in the city centre. Their preferred suburbs and dwelling areas are within sight and easy reach of it. Everyone's ambition is to own a boat of some kind, and to sail on its broad, uncluttered surface.

For it is a superb boating harbour, big enough not to be too crowded with the shipping of commerce, sheltered by Rangitoto and, farther out on the Hauraki Gulf, Waiheke Island's larger bulk, and protected from the madder moods of the Pacific Ocean by the long finger of Coromandel Peninsula and the huge hump of Great Barrier Island.

New Zealanders generally tend to believe that Auckland is the place where it's all happening; and indeed, there are theatres, raceways, sportsgrounds, a sub-tropical climate, (bananas grow in Auckland), and an overall impression of a loud and colourful life.

If Auckland sprawls leisurely about her wandering harbour, Wellington crowds closely about hers, leaning over it, dabbling her toes in it, borrowing some of its ample

area on which to build her commercial centre, a seemingly precarious foothold on a few meagre acres of reclaimed land in which streets are jammed together haphazardly, and little, narrow lanes dart between close-crowded buildings.

Wellington, like Auckland, is easily accessible; by rail, by ferries from Lyttelton and Picton in the South Island, and by air. Its international airport is a minor marvel of engineering, for it juts into the harbour at one end, and into Cook Strait at the other; a whole, large, bulky hill, covered with houses, had to be removed in the course of its construction.

Wellington knew the high-rise building before Auckland did, and erected office blocks like towers—for a different reason. I suspect that Auckland's tallest buildings were always marks of her affluence and opulence, whereas Wellington's were born of necessity. For Wellington is the country's capital, and therefore the administrative centre of New Zealand. Here are the head offices of many of its biggest corporations, its insurance companies and its banks. All of them have to crowd on to that slim strip of reclaimed land, where the main thoroughfare still follows the curve of the original beach, and still retains the name, Lambton Quay, though it is now mostly three blocks from the wharves. Head-office buildings couldn't, therefore, spread out. They had to go upwards.

Wellington and Mount Victoria

Wellington's business and administrative heart crowds around the harbour, its growing office and hotel buildings and commercial development blocks gradually pushing out the fringe of older residential housing. The principal wharves are from centre to centre left in this view. The large wharf in the middle distance is the overseas terminal, where passengers from overseas liners disembark unencumbered by the traffic of the cargo wharves.

Bottom left: *Boat Harbour, Oriental Bay, Wellington*

Wellington harbour offers splendid boating water. Land-locked and surrounded by the city on its steep hillsides, the harbour possesses numerous sandy bays, the nearest of which to the city centre is Oriental Bay, a delightful stretch of wave-lapped sand mere minutes from the commercial heart of Wellington. The boat harbour lies between the beach and the base of the Overseas Terminal wharf.

Bottom right: *Blossom and Daffodils, Hagley Park*

Hagley Park is divided into two main sections, between which runs the main road from Riccarton to town. This section of the road passes through woodland, mostly English trees, with plantings of cherries and other blossom trees. In springtime, commuters on the red Christchurch buses ride in to work past these delightful glades, a blaze of green and white and gold.

Opposite top: *Westhaven Sunrise, Auckland*

It is the ambition of almost every Aucklander to own some sort of small boat, which is not surprising in view of the ideal conditions offered by the harbour, and the opportunities for deep-water sailing out in the Hauraki Gulf, with its many islands. Westhaven is one of a number of small-boat harbours around the shores of the Waitemata.

Opposite bottom: *Southern Alps and Christchurch from Cashmere*

From the hillside suburb of Cashmere, superb views are obtained of the plains and the distant mountains. The suburb seen spread across the plain in this view is Halswell, south-easternmost of the Christchurch residential areas. In the distance is Wigram Air Base, one of the birthplaces of New Zealand aviation and still a Royal New Zealand Air Force base.

Wellington has, for many years, crushed into that tiny space, with its residential sections climbing and clambering up alarming gradients on the surrounding high hills, where they still perch like seabirds on rocky platforms in the midst of unmolested patches of original bush and runaway acreages of pioneer-planted gorse.

Ultimately, the city had to break out, and the cable car, (there is just one pair, on one double track), opened up the hinterland. Land which had been lying vacant behind that first range of formidable ridges was now cleared for building. It was at last a viable proposition to build a home there, for now the city and one's place of business were mere minutes away.

Even so, westward expansion is still limited by the difficulty of building on steep, slip-prone hills, and eastward expansion is even more difficult because of the bush-clad Orongorongo Range, which rears up a stone's throw from the harbour shore. The overflow of Wellington's population of workers is now accommodated in Petone, Wellington's twin city which begins at the harbour-head beach and spreads northwards up the Hutt Valley. Or it lives in the one-time satellite town and now virtual suburb of Johnsonville, in a fold in the hills, reached by the Ngauranga Gorge, or by a railway which darts in and out of the tunnels which pierce the granite hills. More still are housed in the dormitory city of Porirua, thirty odd kilometres up the north-west coast. Wellington proper, therefore, is unlikely to grow much bigger in terms of area, which makes it a manageable, pleasant city to live in.

By and large, it is not a city of quarter-acre sections with well-tended gardens, because the nature of the terrain precludes any such arrangement over much of its area. But it is something which is perhaps more beautiful. Once you get out of the city centre and into the suburbs—Kelburn and Karori in particular—you find yourself in a city-in-a-forest. Steep sections are still thick with original growth of native bush, with long flights of steps leading up from the streets to the half-hidden houses. Here and there, in newer and flatter suburbs, the familiar quarter-acre section with its formal garden is

Hamilton City from Hamilton Lake Domain ▼

Hamilton is an inland city, principal town of the Waikato, in the Auckland Province, and one of the fastest-growing of all New Zealand cities. Straddling the Waikato River, it is beginning to sprawl across the rich Waikato landscape. An attractive city, blessed by a mild climate, it features some beautiful residential areas bordering Hamilton Lake, tree-shaded and bird-haunted, with huge Monarch butterflies fluttering amid bright gardens.

Dunedin City and Octagon ▶

The Octagon is Dunedin's city centre. In fact, the gardened and tree-shaded area to which the name has become attached is not as true an octagon as the streets which run one block out from the centre—but the central area is nevertheless beautiful, with its Robert Burns statue, (that indispensible furnishing of any truly Scottish city), and the Gothic facade of the Anglican Cathedral standing at the head of a broad flight of steps. The Town Hall balconies look out over the Octagon, and from here historic announcements and royalty and other notables have been heard by great crowds. The area slopes gently to the sun.

apparent, a splash of contrivance in the midst of natural artlessness; but the overall impression is of tree-screened houses on hillsides.

Wellington is ˜tending to be a city of architectural extremes—the avant-garde beside the Victorian and Edwardian; houses perched on dizzy tops and ledges overlooking homes set in delightful valleys and dells.

It's all quite unlike Christchurch, second largest city in New Zealand. Christchurch has half the population of Auckland, but sprawls over almost as great an area. Like all South Island towns, it is rather better planned than the North Island cities, because it was planned down to the finest detail by its founders before its first citizens ever set foot

in New Zealand. Maori-Pakeha relations in the South Island were generally good which made the purchase of land easier. The land on which Christchurch was built is billiard-table flat, and the immigration planning included the bringing out of sufficient artisans and labourers to implement the plan properly.

Christchurch is a four-square sort of city. Its main streets are generally wide and straight, and cross one another at precise right angles. It is said to be an 'English' city, with its Gothic Revival cathedral sited dead centre, in the city square, and its remarkable Provincial Council Chamber, relic of the days when each province had its own government, and built like a little West-

minster, its earlier portion, holding ministerial offices, in wood, and the later Council Chamber, for all the world like the House of Commons and containing the finest barrel-vaulted ceiling in the southern hemisphere, in locally quarried stone. It stood on the banks of the pretty Avon stream, when first erected, alone and splendid, surrounded by the newly formed streets and precious few other buildings, a mark of the self-confidence of the colonists.

Christchurch is beautiful, in places. Like all cities, its industrial areas are drab at best, hideously scruffy at worst; but its older residential sections, particularly in the north-western quarter, are places of gracious homes of all sizes, tree-shaded and surrounded by proud gardens and venerable oaks, elms and limes. The Avon River, flowing through the heart of the city, is bordered by smooth lawns and fine garden plots, and is bridged by a number of graceful bridges, many of them little Victorian gems, with their lace-like wrought iron railings painted a fresh white and blue.

Part of Christchurch climbs into the hills of Banks Peninsula. Here is the old-established but still growing suburb of Cashmere, with its native trees and bluegums and its maze of winding streets; or the hills overlooking the estuary of the Avon and Heathcote Rivers, and the prodigious sweep of Pegasus Bay. Houses here perch high on ledges of volcanic rock, and cliffs are draped, in summer, with red-and-purple ice plant.

Lombardy Poplars in Autumn Colour, Avon River

The Avon, when the settlers arrived, was a swampy creek. One of their first tasks was to barber it into a pleasant, free-flowing waterway, navigable for small coastal schooners for some distance. In the course of time, the banks were gardened and trees, including these magnificent Lombardy poplars, planted. A city businessman gave, early this century, a long stretch of concrete balustrading, complete with landing stages and rings for tying up boats and punts, with a fine colonnaded bandstand, still used for Sunday night concerts, and a nearby concrete shelter. Punts have gone out of fashion, but the embankment, shaded by poplars, is still very beautiful.

Christchurch is a city of small theatres, including two very fine theatres in its new Town Hall complex. It is a place of immense parks, such as Hagley Park, with its formal gardens, its golf course, its sports grounds and its woodlands, all right in the centre of the city, and guarded zealously, not to say jealously, by Christchurch citizens. The Christchurch International Airport is the country's finest, being capable of indefinite expansion in almost any direction, for Christchurch is situated on the Canterbury Plains.

Christchurch sprawls, as Auckland does; but here the sprawl is somewhat undesirable, since the city is swallowing up fertile farmland at an alarming rate. Yet the city still possesses this charming characteristic, that you can be driving along through a densely populated area, street after street of bungalows—and, suddenly, you turn a corner, and you're in the midst of quiet farmland, where tall poplars and dark *macrocarpa* grow, and cows stand somnolently in their shade. You take another turn, and you're in the city again.

It also has the advantage of stretching along kilometres of safe, sandy beach, where the surf is good and the water sparklingly clean.

Dunedin, fourth of New Zealand's four 'main centres', is frankly Victorian. This is not to say that it is lacking in amenities of the most up-to-date kind. Indeed, it has some very fine, very modern hotels, is a centre of considerable artistic and cultural activity; but it has many substantial mansions, built and occupied at a time when many North Island centres were rude collections of *raupo* huts—and the delightful thing is that they are still occupied, in many cases, by the families whose forebears built them. Wellington's Victorian and Edwardian villas are most usually divided inside into a number of flats; but those proud old houses in Dunedin are still, more often than not, family homes.

Dunedin, like Wellington, is a city in a forest. It is possible to take winding drives around its steep hillsides, along broad streets with paved footpaths and good lighting, and see very few houses. They are there, all right, but are hidden in little, leafy islands of peace and quiet. Five minutes from the city centre, there are areas of exquisite and unspoiled beauty, a green belt which has every intention of remaining a green belt, and will probably do so for ages to come. For Dunedin is conservative in the best sense of the word. Progress for the sake of progress is not its way. There's a strong strain of good Scottish commonsense which builds where building is clearly required, and tears down where neither use nor pleasure can reasonably be expected any more.

Dunedin, like Christchurch, has its clean, sandy beaches, Ocean Grove, St Kilda and St Clare, with others on the ocean side of the Otago Peninsula reachable by some fairly precipitous roads.

Of the provincial centres, there are coastal cities like New Plymouth, Tauranga and Napier in the North Island, and inland towns such as Hamilton and Palmerston North, and, in the South Island, Blenheim and Ashburton.

Coastal cities, generally speaking, were centres of earliest European settlement. Inland cities, as might be expected, were founded much later.

Hamilton, for example, was founded around 1864, originally as two towns, both military settlements occupied by Fencibles, the 4th Waikato Regiment, an army of occupation following the expulsion of adherents of the Maori King. Each man was given 50 acres to farm, and a one-acre town section. They built redoubts on either side of the Waikato River, and the settlements that grew up around them were known as Hamilton East and Hamilton West. Eventually, of course, a substantial bridge made traffic between the two villages safer, and the two settlements became one.

Christchurch Town Hall

Opened in 1973, the Christchurch Town Hall complex has won acclaim from overseas visitors. Containing two excellent theatres, a restaurant and administrative offices, the building stands on the banks of the Avon, partially screened by venerable willows, except where the fountain plays in a pool slightly raised above the placid Avon.

Hamilton today is a rapidly growing business centre, with its university, its factories and its sprawling housing. The administrative centre of some of the richest dairying land in the world, it is a thriving, bustling place, which has managed to retain much of its beauty. The riverbank is attractively laid out, and Hamilton Lake is a tree-bordered reach of placid water where swans glide and ducks bring up large families.

New Plymouth is an older settlement—not quite a quarter of a century older. It is a seaside town, hilly and pleasant, with its older part still clinging close to the waterfront, its street pattern tending to be four-square, as befits a planned town, but with wandering ways cutting diagonally across the orderly squares, or wandering beside a brawling little stream, probably because the settlers, with some disregard for the schemes of the planners, insisted on taking the easiest path between two points rather than the direct one. Also, New Plymouth was under seige in 1860, and it is possible that some of the city's ways were the shortest paths to defence points about the perimeter. Whereas Hamilton was intended from the first as a garrison town, New Plymouth became one because of the fortunes of war. Its lovely old St Mary's stone church, with its pillars carved from whole *puriri* trees, and its brass plaques expressing gratitude for sanctuary during the troubled times, still bears around its nave the hatch-

Top: Orchards near Hastings

Poplar-lined paddocks and orchards are a familiar sight in Hawkes Bay. Hastings, the 'fruit bowl of New Zealand', is an important fruit and vegetable processing town.

◄ *Civic Square, Palmerston North*

A pleasant inland city on the Manawatu Plain, Palmerston North has become an important educational and cultural centre.

ments of many famous British regiments, and the colours of famous New Zealand regiments which were born in those times.

Life in these provincial centres is pleasant. There is not the crush and hustle of a metropolis, yet there are entertainments and cultural activities, and most of the amenities one associates with a modern western-style city. They are still undoubtedly big small-towns, with their shopping centres still confined to a specific downtown area, wherein everyone shops at least once a week; and they retain that degree of civic pride which is the mark of the small-town community. They are entities, not too big to grasp. The inhabitants, far from knowing everyone in town as can be the case in a very small town, are at least aware of everyone. And they have an identity. They are Hamilton people, or New Plymouth people. This is passing, in the larger centres. In Auckland, people tend to be North Shore people, or Devonport people, or Onehunga (pronounce it Oh-knee-hunga) people. Wellingtonians, those who live in Wellington itself, are definitely and happily Wellingtonians; but, of course, many of the people working in Wellington don't happen to live there, and many who do live there happen to have come to Wellington on transfer within their firm or department, and still regard themselves as Hastings or Waipukurau people. In Christchurch, the citizens in the older suburbs—Riccarton, Woolston, Fendalton, St Albans, Merivale, Papanui, Spreydon, Cashmere—regard themselves as Christchurch people; but people in the newer suburbs, where Christchurch has flowed out into the countryside—Bishopdale, Hornby, Halswell, Upper Riccarton—seem to be assuming an almost separate identity, and the old small-town spirit is fading.

Dunedin people, of course, are Dunedin people; but even here there is evidence that the city has become a collection of suburbs and fringe settlements.

New Zealanders generally have been a small-town people with a small-town outlook and culture. It is rapidly becoming less true of them. The very smallest towns no longer seem to be regarded as places in which people are born, live their lives and die. They are, at most, dormitories. Of those who live in them, many look with some longing towards the cities, believing that there is where it is all happening. If they can't often go to the city, they still live an intensely urban life vicariously, through the media of television, radio and cinema. Many of the smallest rural communities are decaying. But the larger country towns, places like Rangiora, Waimate, Marton, Kaitaia, are still great places to live, proud of their achievements and the good life they offer. The towns are trimmed and barbered and full of community activity.

Our greatest men and women, our leaders in almost every field, have been small-town people, more often than not. I rather think that it is because of our small-town outlook and attitudes that New Zealand has often been a world leader in, for instance, some aspects of social legislation. We've never, even in our largest cities, been so big that people have become mere statistics. But—it's beginning to happen. There is room for a great many more small towns of from two to ten thousand population. I hope we build them, and refuse to allow our cities to grow any larger.

◀ *Wanganui City and River*

Wanganui is an attractive city situated five kilometres upstream from the river mouth, amidst rolling sheep and beef country.

New Plymouth and Mount Egmont ▼

New Plymouth clusters about the foreshore as if, like the original settlers, it is reluctant to push inland. New suburbs, however, are now thrusting in to the deep, bush-filled rifts and the green hillsides behind the city proper. New Plymouth has some delightful parks and public gardens, from any one of which breathtaking vistas of dark hills and the cone of Mount Egmont may be obtained through a frame of native bush.

The wilderness tamed

New Zealand has been settled, successively and at no very remote period, by three distinct types of immigrant.

The first were the Moa Hunters, arriving probably about the 10th century A.D., from Pacific islands, notably Tahiti. They made little mark on the land, and appear to have been hunter-gatherers, content to harvest the rich bounty of the sea, and to hunt the *moa*, a flightless grazing bird, the largest species of which were about the size of a large emu.

The later arrivals, who came in what is spoken of traditionally as the Great Fleet Migration, were more vigorous and considerably more aggressive. They cultivated plots of land, whereon they planted *kumara*, a type of sweet potato; yet they were, in a sense, nomadic, for they moved seasonally from cultivations to bird forest to eel weir and duck lake to the coast, within certain prescribed tribal boundaries. Their greatest land-shaping efforts were in the field of military engineering, at which they were supremely gifted. (In later clashes with Europeans, they built fortresses which were proof against the heaviest artillery of the day, and so riddled with tunnels and hidden ways that, even if the enemy did manage to enter them, large bodies of warriors could pop up in their rear, with devastating results.) Many a hilltop still shows plainly the

trenching and terracing of fortified villages.

The European arrived, bent upon re-creating for himself the kind of homeland that he had left behind. He built his towns, and he worked with axe and firestick to clear vast areas of virgin forest for use as farmland. He made a considerable impression on the land, not only in the amount of it which was once bush and is now pasture, but also in the erosion he caused because he didn't understand the part that bush plays in holding hillsides firm under the seasonally heavy rainfall.

So many of the steeper tracts of hill country are today scarred by massive slips, and much formerly useful land has acquired a coat of gorse which is rather more dense and much more difficult to eradicate than it is in England, from where the first fatal seeds were imported.

But, on the credit side, the pioneer worked the land, and did it well. I have diary pages written by my grandfather in the 1860s, which are chiefly interesting for the insight which they give into the way in which farming practice changed in a relatively short period. It changed, quite clearly, from the secure, hedged-field husbandry of England, with its flocks numbered in mere hundreds, to the management of flocks numbering thousands, spread over a countryside which was steep, with swamps in its

Pastoral, near Lawrence

Lawrence, in South Otago, was the site of perhaps the most famous and prolific of all New Zealand gold-rush scrambles, at Gabriel's Gully. Newly-arrived fossickers, rooting up tussock clumps on the hills in

this vicinity, found sizeable nuggets clinging to the roots. Today, the rolling, green hills carry sheep, and the clang of pick and shovel and the roar of sluices are no longer heard, though it is still possible to pan creeks in the area and win a little colour.

Mount Peel Station and Cabbage Tree ▲

Mount Peel Station is typical of Canterbury back-country sheep runs. The station spreads itself over high hills which are snow-covered during winter, and penetrates far into the foothill ranges up long river valleys. The cabbage tree in the foreground is common in this area and throughout most of pastoral New Zealand. Though having the appearance of a branched palm, it is actually a relation of the lily.

◄ *Four Peaks from Mount Michael, Canterbury*

Reaching up towards the high country, but not so high as to be in tussock or snowgrass country, this back-country station is green and tamed, with orderly wind-breaking shelterbelts and green grasses and clovers abounding.

Arrow Basin ▶

Sheep farming in the Southern Lakes area was begun early in the 1860s, and received an initial boost by having a ready local market in the form of gold-seekers, who flocked to the area in 1863. The climate is one of fairly harsh extremes, which is evident in the arid, rocky aspect of much of the country; but the river valleys, like that of the Arrow River, are fertile and forgiving, and produce good pasture.

hollows and bush in its hanging valleys, and was measured in square miles rather than mere acres. There is mention of blade shearing, with a suspicion of surprise at the time the operation took, and the size of the clip. There is talk of going out and bringing the flock in to sheltered paddocks near the homestead when the weather became rough; and there's a wealth of details of such practices as rubbing rum or brandy on to a ewe's face when persuading her to accept an orphan lamb as her own.

Gradually, the attitudes and practices changed. Gradually the emphasis changed from keeping the new settlements in meat and milk, to selling meat, wool and tallow overseas, mainly to England. Farming became less a matter of subsistence and more a matter of business, and big business, at that.

More and more land was taken up by sheep farmers, and would-be sheep farmers. Dynasties were founded, their fortunes made and assured for years to come, their influence powerful. The farms continued to support the towns, but by the trade they created rather than by the food they supplied.

New Zealand is still very much a sheep country. Cattle are becoming more important, but are still largely raised and fattened as a second string, by sheep men. There are rich dairy areas, notably the Waikato, just to the south of Auckland, and Taranaki, on the West Cape. Dairy farms, until comparatively recently, have been small operations. A small sheep farm, in most areas, would be 280 to 400 hectares. A small dairy farm could be as small as forty hectares; and until perhaps thirty years ago, its produce was consumed by three main markets—cheese factory, butter factory and town milk supply; and even the cheese and butter factories found the greatest market for their produce locally. Today, New Zealand cheese is winning customers in many markets overseas. From a pale yellow cheddar and a slightly orange-coloured process cheese, the range has grown to include blues, smoked cheeses and counterparts of practically every major type of cheese made in Europe or the United States. Butter exports are high, and milk powder, condensed milk and other milk forms and products have won good markets. Dairy farms, therefore, are tending to be larger than they were. Herds have increased since the advent of mechanical milking, and sheds are more sophisticated.

The dairy industry is spread all over New Zealand, (the Waikato and Taranaki being merely the largest areas given over almost entirely to dairying), the main requirement being a good rainfall and country which is not too steep.

High-country sheep stations are generally enormous—hundreds of square kilometres. Many are still huge stations, but on some of them, notably Molesworth in the Marlborough back country, in the heart of the mountains, sheep farming has been abandoned in favour of cattle. Sheep are close grazers and have in the past eaten the heart out of Molesworth. Aerial topdressing and careful pasture rehabilitation and management have transformed the almost desert region into good grazing once more—this time for beef cattle.

Little cereal farming is carried on. The pioneers grew their own wheat and milled it to provide their own flour. The importation of better wheats, notably from Australia, made cereal farming less profitable, and in those flat, alluvial areas where it was once a principal agricultural activity, it has tended to give way to sheep farming. Quite large areas of oats are still sown and harvested, but the golden seas of grain which once clothed the Canterbury Plains, for instance, are gone, and the land is now mostly pasture.

Fields on the Canterbury Plains ▲

The mosaic-like pattern of fields reflects the carving up of squatters' land during the 1880s. Shelter belts protect the mixed crops from the dry nor'-wester.

Mustering, Glen Tanner Station, Mount Cook ▶

The brown, snowgrass-covered country about the feet of the high Alps has an almost desert-like aspect; but it has proved eminently suitable for raising vast flocks of Merino sheep and Merino-based crossbreeds. High, rugged peaks are grazed over in the summer, but the sheep are brought down to the flats for the winter.

Tulip Farm, Waimate ▶

Immigrant Dutch horticulturalists have established themselves in market flower gardens here and there on the Canterbury Plain.

◀ *Kerikeri, Northland*

It was in this area that the first plough turned the first furrow in New Zealand, in the 1820 s. Agriculture began here, and was well rewarded, for the soil is rich and the climate warm and gentle—one of those blessed places where you 'tickle the earth with a hoe and it laughs a harvest'. Today fruit, especially citrus, is grown here.

Tarawera Farmlands ▼

Typical of the land around the Rotorua area and the great volcanic fault-line, the Tarawera landscape alternated between deep, rift-like, forested valleys and rugged hills, and gentler pasture country, where the grass grows green and lush in the humid climate and rich volcanic soil.

 The Ruahine Ranges near Dannevirke

Pohangina Valley ▶

Typical of central North Island sheep country, this steeply ridged land is seamed with the tracks of sheep along its green faces. Once covered with dense forest, it still protects pockets of bush in its valleys.

Mount Egmont Landscape, Taranaki, North Island ▼

Fairly high annual rainfall and a mild climate combine to make Taranaki farmlands exceptionally rich. Renowned as much for its fine cheeses as its scenes of exquisite pastoral beauty, Taranaki is dominated by Mount Egmont, from whose Maori title the province takes its name.

In the matter of size of sheep farms, Canterbury seems to be the exception which proves the rule. It is, for eighty kilometres north from Ashburton, a place of small farms of forty to eighty hectares. There are exceptions, but the small farms are more common here than anywhere else in the country. They tend to be mixed farms, running sheep, but also producing potatoes, peas, barley, oats and lucerne. From the air, therefore, the plains present a variegated patch-work not seen anywhere else in the country—kilometre after kilometre of green, buff, brown and gold fields, patched by dark pine shelter belts, and divided by vast irrigation races which, tapping the waters of both the rain- and snow-fed rivers, ensure a year-round adequate supply of water.

Canterbury often strikes the visitor as a treeless area. It isn't, as it happens, but there are large areas of flat paddocks, merely patched with what appear to be high, dark hedges, and which are actually shelter brakes of pine, kept neatly trimmed by means of a Heath-Robinson contraption of whirling blades mounted on a tractor. These shelter belts have the important function of breaking the force of the mad nor'wester, a hot sirocco of a wind which romps across the plains with gale force, particularly between September and November.

From Timaru south, the land becomes hilly, and is largely sheep country. It is generally greener here where the land gradually begins to heave itself up towards the foothills of the Alps. It rolls on down to the very edge of the ocean, perching its little townships on river banks.

North Otago hills are equally high, lowering and standing back from the coast around the Waitaki River, and forming a broad, flat plain briefly near Oamaru before becoming humped and high again. This, also, is sheep farming country. In fact, the first shipments of frozen mutton were sent to England from Otago.

Sheep and cattle farming, and some dairying, is the major industry from here south, to Invercargill. In places (such as South Otago's Catlins district), there is a pioneer quality of life, where farms are still being won from heavy forest; but the clearing is no longer haphazard or ill-considered. Farms are often divided by arms of forest, preserved to keep the hills intact and the rich topsoil from being carried down to the rivers.

Cattle are farmed on the narrow coastal strip of Westland, and valiant battles are being fought to prevent some of the fiercer rivers from inundating the farmland, not with water alone, but with gravel and boulders, spoil ripped from the flanks of the mountains by the powerful waters.

To the north, the pattern is not too dissimilar. Northland, which long held the reputation of being a scrubby neck of land, swampy and covered with the pits and scarpings of the hordes of gum diggers who sought the highly-prized *kauri* gum, is really not a bit like that. The almost sub-tropical climate of the Bay of Islands encourages growth. Kerikeri is a fruit-growing centre, mostly citrus fruit, but with apples, tamarillos

and other fruit being produced in quantity. It is a landscape of reddish, tilled earth bordered by intensely green hedges.

Much of the rest of the peninsula is given over to dairy farming, sheep farming on the rolling, central heights, and the country's only remaining *kauri* forests. The *kauri* is a magnificent tree, a sort of antipodean Cedar of Lebanon, with its straight bole, branchless to a considerable height. Great inroads were made into the *kauri* forests of Northland in the nineteenth century, which is understandable, when you look at the trees. They must have made admirable masts and yards for shipping; and the durability of *kauri* timber is legendary. There are trees in those forests

Middlepark Stud, Near Cambridge ▲

Favourably compared with Kentucky Blue Grass country, Cambridge has produced some very fine racehorses and bloodstock.

◀ *Cattle Farming, Karapiro*

Lake Karapiro, in the rich Waikato district, is a man-made lake which was formed by the damming of the Waikato River (part of a hydro-electric scheme). The principal industries hereabouts are beef-cattle and dairy farming, with some stud farming, including the raising and training of racehorses.

which were quite tall youngsters when Jesus walked the earth, and when you cut a good tree down, you cut down two to three thousand years of growth. It takes a long time to replace, which is why the forests are protected today.

There is a seemingly vast forest on the western side of the peninsula, the Waipoua State Forest. But it isn't so vast, really. Some 1 600 hectares of *kauri* and other indigenous trees is a pathetic remnant of the great forests of *kauri* that once covered the land.

The land immediately surrounding Auckland tends to vary from the hummocky swampiness around Helensville to the bush-covered splendour of the Waitakere Ranges. In between those two extremes there is the wine-growing area in the Henderson Valley, heavy, clay soil of which the founder of a local winery said, quoting an old Lebanese proverb: 'The vine shall redeem the waste places of the earth'.

And it has indeed. Some superb wines are produced in this area today.

The Waikato, drained and watered by its great river, and once patched with immense swamps, has always been rich land. Today it is tamed into highly productive dairy land in the south-west, and equally fine sheep country in the north-east. In the days before the Kingite Wars, the Maoris, profiting by the lessons of the missionaries, turned it into their granary. Wheat grew here in prodigious crops. Peaches, almonds, apples, and all manner of vegetables were cultivated. It is still some of the richest soil in New Zealand.

The volcanic plateau for long remained a virtual desert. The acid pumice soil was too poor to support sheep or cattle adequately,

and would not grow very much more than the coarse *manuka* scrub that still patches much of it. The radiata pine, however, thrives in it. In the early 1930s, during the depression, relief workers found jobs planting seedlings by hand, and these have grown at a rate unequalled anywhere else in the world. Today, vast forests of pine cover the land with dark green, tossing verdure, and the plateau supports a great forest farming and milling industry, producing timber and paper.

On the east coast of the North Island, Hawkes Bay and the Wairarapa, once heavily timbered, are now gently rolling sheep and cattle country, with the main accent on sheep.

Exotic Forest, Kinleith ▲

In the sour pumice soils of the volcanic plateau, exotic trees, mostly radiata pine, are farmed for pulp and paper manufacture. In an area of man-made forest such as this, as much as 12 000 hectares may be clearfelled each year, and 400 hectares replanted.

◀ *Kauri Trees, Waipoua State Forest*

After years of unchecked exploitation, the remnants of once-vast *kauri* forests were protected by law. Waipoua State Forest, where these trees are growing, contains several venerable giants in its 16 000 hectares. Perhaps the best known is *Tane Mahuta*, 'God of the Forest', thirteen metres in girth, with its lowest branches some twelve metres from the ground.

Benmore State Hydro-electric Scheme ▲

One of the largest earth dams, and the largest single power-producing station in the Southern Hemisphere, Benmore is some 110 metres high and 610 metres long. Behind it, the Waitaki River has backed up to form New Zealand's largest man-made lake, inundating some seventy-seven square kilometres of high-country farmland. Trees now grow along stretches of lake shore, and the effect of the large body of water on the local climate has been marked. The brown tussock and desert-like appearance of much of the lakeside landscape has given way to green, lush pasture, uncharacteristic of this part of the country.

Whakamaru Dam ▶

Whakamaru is one of a series of dams which make up the vast hydro-electric scheme on the Waikato River, a 'managed' river resource from the Lake Taupo to the Waikato Heads.

It's a crumpled country, with rounded hills and quiet rivers, and three more or less flat stretches—the Heretaunga Plain, dotted with orchards, patched with *raupo* swamps and laced with placid streams; Takapau Plain, narrow, long, slightly humped and edged by the willow-bordered Tukituki River, where sheep and dairy cows graze, and cereal crops are grown; and the wide, flat valley between the Aorangi and Rimutaka Ranges, spreading out as it comes down to Cook Strait, past the broad, shallow waters of Lake Wairarapa and Lake Ferry Lagoon, mostly sheep country, though with some dairying and, around Greytown and Carterton, broad acreages of orchards.

This more-or-less easy, exceedingly fertile pastoral land is separated from the rough, often soggy lowlands south of the Manawatu by country which is not so much crumpled as sharply creased and heavily forested, much of it a wilderness where deer and wild pig roam, (and are hunted), in hidden valleys and alongside bush-shaded river flats.

The 'backblocks' farms reach cleared and grassed fingers deep into this complex of valleys and ridges, and sheep graze paddocks which are still strewn with scatterings of recently cleared bush. Strategic stands of timber hold the hill faces firm against erosion; and, indeed, the worst erosion is still seen to be in the high country east of the ranges, where an earlier generation of frontier farmers cleared incautiously, ignorant of the effects of high rainfall on precipitously steep hillsides deprived of the reinforcing network of great root systems, and the umbrella-like protection of high foliage.

The coastal farms tend to be hummocky, with a water table never far below the surface, and with increasingly broad acreages of sand dunes as the coast sweeps up towards the Wanganui River. It is dairying country, too footwet for sheep. Flax has been grown here, and flaxmills were once common; but improved drainage, while increasing the available grazing land, has done away with the swamps in which *Formium tenax*, the coarse New Zealand flax, used to grow.

Vast areas of New Zealand are set aside as National Parks, where New Zealanders and overseas visitors can enjoy the different types of scenery and wildlife that the country offers. Several million hectares are preserved in this way, the largest being Fiordland National Park, with over one and a quarter million hectares, and the second largest the Urewera National Park, (containing the very lovely Lake Waikaremoana), 2 000 square kilometres of mountainous rainforest country, with deep river valleys and high, misty peaks.

Ferns ▶

◀ *Tarawera Landscape*

New Zealand ferns comprise a wide variety of species, from the great tree ferns such as *Cyathea medullaris* and *Dicksonia squarrosa* to the tiny Filmy Fern, with fronds sometimes only one cell thick. Ferns of this type, *Blechnum discolor*, feature prominently as an element of Maori art, its curved shoots recurring again and again as a carving motif.

◀ Mountain Daisy

There are fifty-eight species of Mountain Daisy found in New Zealand, of which these are probably the most familiar. They grow, as the name suggests, in alpine regions, and are large and very showy.

The Kiwi ▲

New Zealand's national emblem, the Kiwi, is a flightless bird, occurring in four main species, three of which are strictly nocturnal. These are the North Island Kiwi, which is the bird most frequently depicted as the country's emblem; the South Island Kiwi, or Tokoeka; the Large Grey Kiwi, or Roa; the Little Grey Kiwi. The Tokoeka which live on Stewart Island are not strictly nocturnal, unlike the others, but may quite often be seen in broad daylight in Stewart Island bush.

Tui on Kowhai Tree

The *tui*, sometimes called the Parson Bird because of the little tuft of white feathers at his throat, is common in forests and reserves throughout New Zealand. About the size of a small raven, with a sheen to his feathers like that of a starling, he is a mimic and a great songster. Most of the singing that falls within the range of the human ear is in the form of clicks, knocking sounds and a bell-like chiming; but his throat can be seen swelling with song too high for the ear to hear.

Kaka Beak

Almost extinct in the wild state, Kaka Beak, (*Clianthus*), was probably saved from extinction by the old-time Maoris, who cultivated it, probably as a source of nectar for caged *tui* birds. The name is derived from the bush parrot, the *kaka*, whose longish, curved bill the flowers resemble. It is seen chiefly as a garden shrub, today.

Mount Cook Lily ▲

Mount Cook Lily, Great Mountain
Buttercup, *Ranunculus lyallii*: three names
to describe a single flower, the best known
of all New Zealand alpine flowers. It is, in
fact, a member of the buttercup family.
New Zealand alpine meadows do not
produce the glorious variety of coloured
blooms which are to be found in a similar
area in Switzerland. They are all white—
but nevertheless, their delicate, waxen
beauty softens an often harsh mountain
landscape.

Kea ▶

The kea, the best-known of New Zealand's
parrots, haunts the snow country of the
South Island.
This cheeky and intelligent bird is
surrounded by controversy as many
runholders believe the kea attacks lambs.

Nature's cauldron – a geothermal wonderland

If you are flying down the east coast of the North Island, over the Bay of Plenty, a little to the south of Tauranga, you'll see White Island, smoking and fuming some kilometres off the mainland shore. And if you look to the starboard side of the aircraft, and the day is fine and clear, you will observe the disturbed land-pattern marking the great volcanic fault-line running through the centre of the North Island, its pathway dotted with extinct, dormant and active volcanoes, steaming lakes, and smoking, steam-wreathed areas of dark scrub and white silica.

It is a weird area, with its warm lakes and its shattered, dead mountains, and it stretches clear from White Island to the central volcanic plateau, pocked and dimpled, with Ruapehu, Tongariro and Ngauruhoe, the three volcanoes, rising up from the wrinkled, seamed earth to the south of Lake Taupo.

At ground level, the netherworldliness of the area is constantly apparent. White Island itself is an uncomfortable place. You reach it by launch from Opotiki, and perhaps wish you hadn't. Here, you keep remembering, men mining sulphur were killed in 1914, in a sudden eruption. You don't wonder at it. You merely wonder what possessed them to stay there at all, for it was then, and is now, a fearsome place, with its snorting fumaroles, its acid lakes and its sulphurous stench.

Sixty to eighty kilometres inland from the mainland coast, a cluster of lakes is set jewel-like in ancient volcanic subsidences— Rotoma, (White or Clear Lake), Rotoehu, (the Bail Lake, or the Lake Shaped like a Canoe Bail), Rotoiti, (Small Lake), and Rotorua, (Lake of the Pit), all fed by cold, rainfed streams which come down through the fissured rock of ancient upheavals, cooled in the shade of the generous rain forest which hides those olden rifts; and they are also fed, here and there, by streams of warm to boiling water, and are occasionally bordered by steaming pools and by whole areas of fumaroles, burbling, slurping, porridge-like boiling mud and spectacular geysers. Farther south, Lake Tarawera spreads over a devastated valley, covering the remains of the once famed Pink and White Terraces, and lapping the shore, at one end of the lake, where the ripped and gashed remains of Mount Tarawera still smoke and tremble. At the other end of the lake, the pathetic remnant of Te Wairoa, once a thriving community and nineteenth century tourist resort, pokes out from the mounded black earth and green grass, known now as Buried Village, and only partially exhumed.

◀ *Steaming Cliffs, Lake Rotomahana.*

◀ *Mount Tarawera Volcanic Rent*

On 10 June, 1886, Mount Tarawera
exploded, destroying the Pink and White
Terraces, killing a large number of people,
and burying the village of Te Wairoa. The
highest peak, today, is that in the centre
foreground, 1 498 metres. At the time of
the eruption, the first explosion burst from
the central peak, after which the entire
mountain split in two. The noise of the
volcano was heard as far away as
Coromandel, a distance of a hundred and
sixty kilometres.

Waimangu Valley and Lake Rotomahana ▲

A sightseeing tour, known as the
'Government Round Trip', leads down
through the awesome Waimangu Valley,
site of the great Warbrick Thermal Terrace,
the Waimangu Geyser (which used to be
the world's biggest, playing 450 metres, but
which is now showing signs of its age), and
by launch across Lake Rotomahana, with
its Steaming Cliffs, to Mount Tarawera
and its six kilometre-long gash.

The lakes in this area are rich in certain minerals, which often distinguish them with vivid colours. On the road to Buried Village, for example, the Blue and Green Lakes lie side by side, separated one from the other by a narrow thread of tree-covered land. The names are apt. Blue Lake is a gem of teal blue, regardless of the colour of the sky at the time of viewing. The colour of Green Lake is simply the green of deep water, beautifully translucent.

The same phenomenon is visible in other waters of the area. The infant Waikato River, running away from Lake Taupo, is astonishingly clear and slightly green-tinted, as though it were made of a kind of liquefaction of sunglass-lenses. Its reflecting power seems somewhat diminished, its clarity greatly enhanced, so that you can see the lithe trout which inhabit it, moving and basking in deep pools, plain to see.

Geothermal activity has been harnessed in the Taupo area, at Wairakei. Great lagged pipes run down the valley in stiff, parallel rows, crossing the main road to the power station, where they turn the generator turbines. The steam pressure is considerable, as it must be for the purpose; and you can find a most convincing example of this at the Karapiti Blowhole nearby, whence steam is seen gushing out ceaselessly, at about 1 268 kilopascals pressure, and has been doing so since before there were men on earth. (It is the thermal region's safety valve.) Even so, the project has not been entirely devoid of difficulty. For one thing, the turbines must operate on an absolutely horizontal floor. To ensure this condition in this tremulous area where earth tremors of one magnitude or another are an almost daily occurrence, the power house has had to be flexible, with walls and floors which can move independently of one another.

But above all else, the thermal area is spectacular. There are geysers which spout boiling water to prodigious heights every day, at the same time, regular as clockwork. There are pits of green, boiling water so deep that their bottoms have never been fathomed. There are places where a man, hammering a stake into the ground, has seen it suddenly disappear, its place taken by a whiff of sulphur and a plume of insubstantial steam. There are spas and warm mineral pools where the arthritic come for, and usually find, relief.

The South Island has one or two thermal areas. There is the Maruia Springs resort, on the Lewis Pass road, in a deep valley surrounded by forested mountains and watered by a broad, gravel-bedded river. There is Hanmer, on the eastern side of those same mountains, where hot mineral waters bubble up from the bowels of the earth and are channelled into baths. There are hot springs at the foot of the Franz Josef Glacier, in Westland.

But pride of place goes to the Rotorua area in the North Island, on that great fault line with its mighty chain of steaming lakes and hot pools of bubbling mud.

◀ *Mount Ngauruhoe from Ruapehu*

The three volcanoes, Ngauruhoe, Tongariro and Ruapehu, smoke and fume high on the North Island's central volcanic plateau. Ngauruhoe is the central peak of the three, a fine symmetrical cone which is actually the offspring of Tongariro, the northernmost volcano, now a shattered series of jagged peaks. Ruapehu, from which this view is obtained, is a truncated cone whose crater contains a steaming lake, the waters of which lap snowy shores around the crater's rim. One of New Zealand's finest skifields is located on Ruapehu.

Mount Ngauruhoe and Lake Taupo ▶

The volcanic origins of the North Island's central plateau are plainly seen in this view of the active volcano, Mount Ngauruhoe, and the nearby gigantic subsidence which forms the bed of Lake Taupo. Here is no slow wrinkling of the earth's crust, but violently-sudden contouring, in geologically-recent times.

Whakarewarewa, Rotorua City and Lake Rotorua ▲

Whakarewarewa, in the foreground, is well named, translating roughly into 'the Valley of Rising Steam'. The area is neatly pathed, and is world famous for its great geysers, its bottomless pools of boiling blue water and its mud and fumaroles. The island on the lake is Mokoia, once the stronghold of the Arawa people. It is also the scene for Maoridom's most famous love story, of Hinemoa and Tutanekai. Tutanekai was a young chief, living on Mokoia Island. Hinemoa was a beautiful maiden living on the mainland shore, and forbidden by her father to see Tutanekai. Tutanekai played his flute one night, and Hinemoa, guided by its music, swam the lake to him.

◄ Warbrick Thermal Terrace, Waimungu

This famous terrace built up of silaceous material layer by layer, is named after a famous Maori guide, Alf Warbrick.

Boiling Mud ▶

Not the least of the fascinations of the thermal areas are the pools of boiling mud. The constantly changing patterns and the colours which vary from chocolate brown to slate grey provide great photographic opportunity; and the activity is sufficiently sluggish to allow a closer approach than is possible with geysers and hot water or steam activities.

◀ *Geothermal Activity, Whakarewarewa*

Pohutu Geyser, Whakarewarewa ▶

One of the most spectacular of the area's geysers, Pohutu plays frequently, hurling steam-plumed jets of boiling water high into the air.

Opposite page:
Mount Ngauruhoe, Tongariro National Park

There is more or less constant activity from Mount Ngauruhoe's crater. Mostly taking the form of a plume of steam, it can erupt with startling vigour and little warning, sending great, billowing clouds of smoke into the sky and powdering the snowfields with ash. Usually, however, some warning is given by its gradually increasing activity.

Bottom: Orakei Korako

Orakei Korako, thirty-odd kilometres north of Taupo, steadily declined as a thermal attraction, its activity diminishing at a rapid rate until, in 1961, a hydro-electric dam across the Waikato River caused the water to back up and form Lake Ohakuri. Immediately, Orakei Korako burst into new life. Principal attractions are Hochstetter Cauldron, ejecting four and a half million litres of boiling water per day; Lady Cobham Geyser; Rainbow Terrace; and the fabulous Golden Fleece.

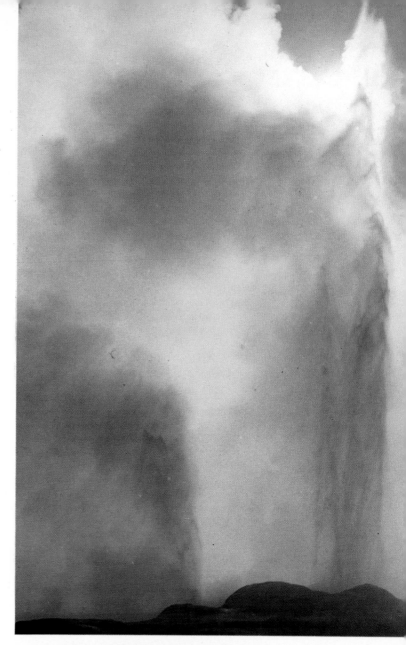

Tongariro National Park and Mount Ngauruhoe

Tongariro National Park was originally presented to the nation by the Chief, Te Heu Heu Tukino. It offers recreational facilities for skiers, trampers, climbers and people who enjoy exploring bush walks and areas of thermal activity.

First published 1975
Reprinted 1976
Revised edition 1977
Reprinted 1978, 1979 and 1980
by Golden Press Pty Ltd
16 Copsey Place
Avondale, Auckland
and
35 Osborne Street
Christchurch
Printed in Hong Kong
ISBN 0 85558 4 327
© Robin Smith and W. Warren Jacobs

We are indebted to Mount Cook Airlines for their generous assistance in air travel, and to the people throughout the country who freely assisted us in many ways

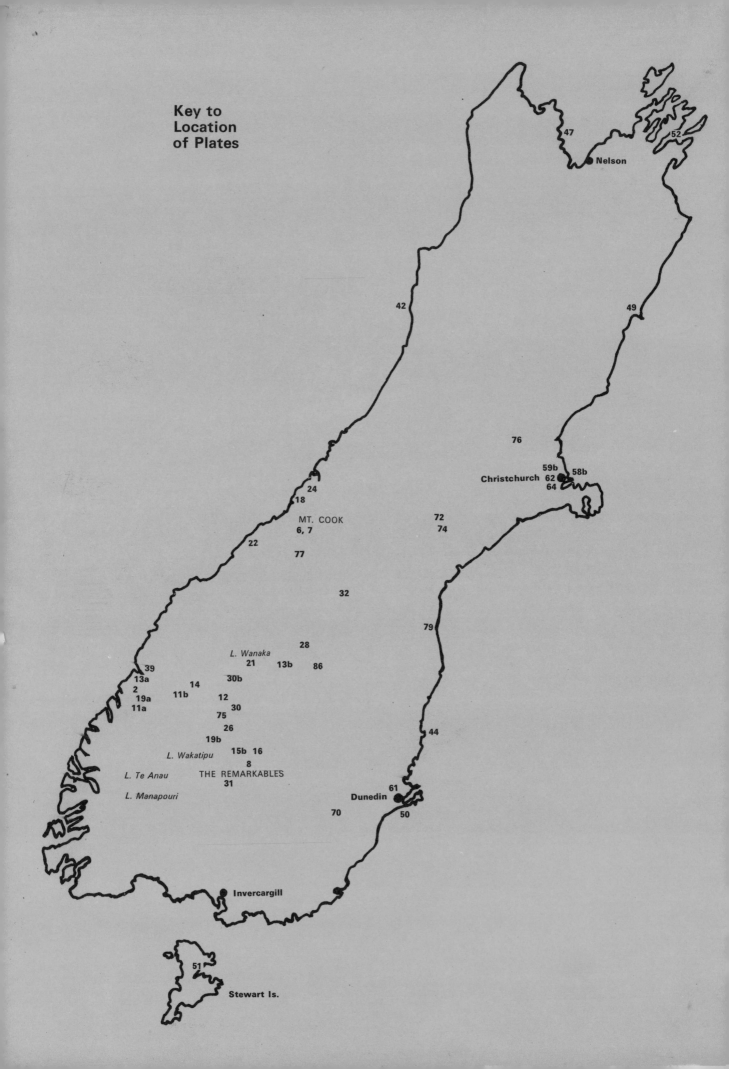

**Key to
Location
of Plates**

47
52
● Nelson

42

49

76

24
18

MT. COOK
6, 7

59b
58b
Christchurch 62
64

72
74

22

77

32

79

28
L. Wanaka
21   13b   86

39
13a
2   14
19a   11b   12
11a

30b

30

75

26

19b

L. Wakatipu   15b 16
8

L. Te Anau   THE REMARKABLES
31

L. Manapouri

44

61
Dunedin
50

70

● Invercargill

51

Stewart Is.